AUSTRALIAN BUTTERFLIES IN STAINED GLASS

Diane Coady

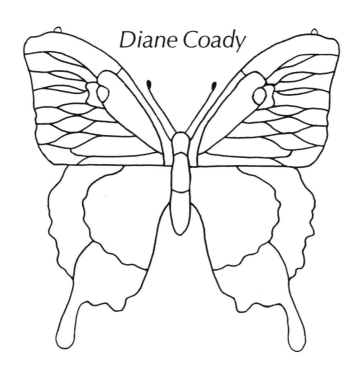

Kangaroo Press

This book of butterfly designs is dedicated to Sarah.

Many thanks to Debbie Lambley for her keyboard expertise.

Glass-ary

Cartoon Full sized line drawing of design

Copper foil Pre-glued narrow strip of fine copper. Also comes in sheets.

Copper foiling Technique using copper foil to hold glass pieces together with solder.

Fid Wooden or plastic tool used with lead and copper foil.

Flux Assists solder to adhere to metal. Can be liquid, cream or solid. As a general rule, flux for lead should not be used for copper.

Glass grinder Machine with a diamond wheel which grinds away small areas of glass. Grinding heads come in assorted sizes.

Lathekin Same as *fid*.

Patina Liquid chemical which alters the colour of silver solder to brass or black.

Polishing compound Liquid polish used to shine glass and solder.

Solder Solid core solder, 60% tin, 40% lead, is known as 60/40 solder; 50% tin, 50% lead solder is called 50/50. More heat is required to melt 50/50 than 60/40.

Stained glass Glass that has been painted or stained, then fired in a kiln. Often used instead of the correct terms, 'leadlight' and 'copper foil'.

Suncatcher Small glass design meant to hang in a window, using natural light to its full advantage.

First published by Kangaroo Press in 1996
3 Whitehall Road Kenthurst NSW 2156 Australia
PO Box 6125 Dural Delivery Centre NSW 2158
Printed in Hong Kong through Colorcraft Ltd

ISBN 0 86417 760 7

Contents

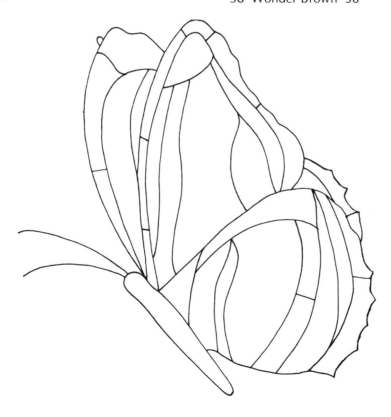

Foreword

Australia is a country of colourful surprises—strange animals, unusual flowers, brilliantly coloured birds and exotic butterflies. Butterflies are usually migratory, but a few do remain in local areas, where their food source is plentiful. All the butterflies in this book are considered native to Australia, although some are found in many other countries as well.

As people become increasingly interested in using nature as a design model for arts and crafts the butterfly is a natural choice as a creative source. I believe Mother Nature was in a whimsical mood when she created butterflies.

This selection of butterfly designs was taken from a range of nearly 400 species. The task of choosing just 38 butterflies was very difficult. The variations within some species complicated my choices even further. My aim was to retain as much of the colour and markings as possible, yet to simplify the butterfly to a practical stained glass design. Some designs are more complicated than others and require more patience, but the beautiful results are well worth the extra effort.

I have drawn most of the butterflies as suncatchers, many with spread wings, some in profile. I have also created a number of patterns combining butterflies and flowers which are suitable for door panels, windows and mirrors. In these patterns you can replace the butterflies I have chosen with any other butterfly you wish. Flower designs to complement the butterflies can be found in my earlier book, *Australian Wildflowers in Stained Glass*.

I hope you enjoy *Australian Butterflies in Stained Glass*.

Diane

Copper Foiling

To reproduce some of the butterfly patterns, a glass grinder with a 6 mm (¼")
diamond head will be required.

1. The patterns have been drawn suncatcher size but can be enlarged, which
will make the butterflies easier to construct. Borders can be added if you wish—
these can be oval, circular or rectangular. The background can be left free of
glass, or filled with clear or coloured glass or mirror (figure 1). Pattern guides
for ovals and circles appear on pages 28-29.

Figure 1

2. A narrow border works best in a darker glass, while a wide border should
be made in a lighter glass.
3. Where you are using background glass, the antennae can be painted on
with black enamel paint or non-fired glass paint. If you have access to a glass
kiln and wish to fire the antennae using kiln-fired paint, remember to do this
before starting to copper-foil that section of the glass.

4. If required, increase the pattern size using a photocopier or the grid method demonstrated in figure 2.

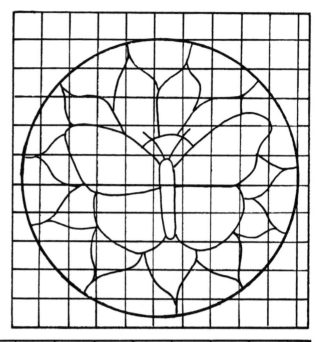

Figure 2 Enlarging by the grid method

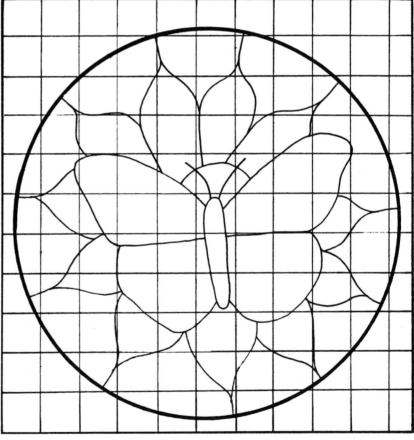

5. Keep to the colour guides as much as possible, remembering not to mix opaque with translucent glass. Butterflies are a great way to use up scraps of glass left over from other projects. Mark directional lines on the pattern if you are using streaky or one-way patterned glass—see figure 3.

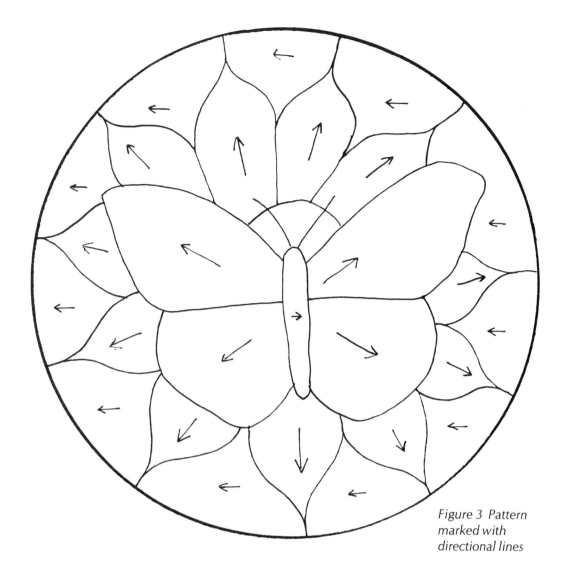

Figure 3 Pattern marked with directional lines

6. Make two copies of the pattern and cover both with a protective layer of clear adhesive plastic to prevent damage from cuts and water. Place one copy on a stearine foam board. This is your 'setting up' pattern. Use the second pattern, the 'working pattern', to cut and grind the glass.

7. Cut and grind each glass section, and place it in position over the pattern on the stearine foam board. Use glass-headed pins to hold the glass firmly in the correct position.

8. When all the glass sections have been cut and ground to fit accurately within the pattern lines, remove the pieces and wash them in warm soapy water. Rinse the pieces to remove any soapy residue. Dry, and then warm the glass pieces with a fan heater or hair dryer. The warmth ensures adhesion of the foil to the glass.

9. Starting at an internal edge, wrap each glass piece with foil, overlapping the join 6 mm (¼"). Press edges down firmly with a fid, or use half a wooden peg. Place each foiled piece in position over the pattern on the stearine foam board and hold in place with the pins. When all the pieces are foiled, flux all the seams and cover with solder. Remove the pins and turn the piece over. Flux and solder the second side.

10. Check that the glass has cooled down! Pick the suncatcher up, and solder the edges. The soldering does not have to be smooth, but all the copper foiling must be covered. Wear protective cloth gloves to prevent hot solder landing on your hands.

11. Wash all the flux away thoroughly with hot soapy water and a sponge, and dry well.

12. Bead-solder all seams and the edge (figure 4).

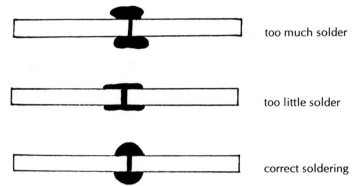

too much solder

too little solder

correct soldering

Figure 4 The right and wrong ways to bead-solder a join

13. To make the antennae and the hanging loop first 'tin' a length of copper wire with flux and apply solder. Use pliers to hold the wire because it conducts heat very quickly. For the antennae cut two lengths of tinned wire slightly longer than the antennae in the pattern. Using needle-nosed pliers bend one end over on each wire piece into matching loops, and fill the centres with solder (figure 5). Touch-solder the antennae in the correct position, using pliers to hold them.

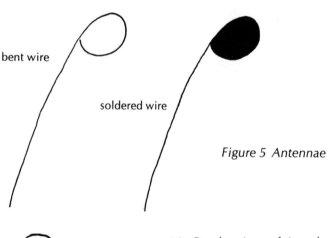

bent wire

soldered wire

Figure 5 Antennae

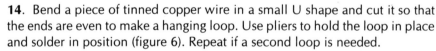

14. Bend a piece of tinned copper wire in a small U shape and cut it so that the ends are even to make a hanging loop. Use pliers to hold the loop in place and solder in position (figure 6). Repeat if a second loop is needed.

Figure 6 Hanging loop

15. Thoroughly wash the completed suncatcher with hot soapy water and a sponge. Remove *all* flux and soldering residue. This is important if the patinaing process is to be successful. Dry the suncatcher with a soft cloth.

16. Remove the pins from the stearine foam board. Wash them in hot soapy water and dry thoroughly to prevent them rusting.

17. The solder can be left silver, or patinaed with brass or black patina. Polish to a high finish using a polishing compound such as Kemp-pro.

18. Use fine nylon fishing line to hang your suncatcher.

THE PATTERNS

1 Amaryllis Azure and Showy Parrot Pea

Illustrated inside front cover

2 Australian Gull

Illustrated inside front cover

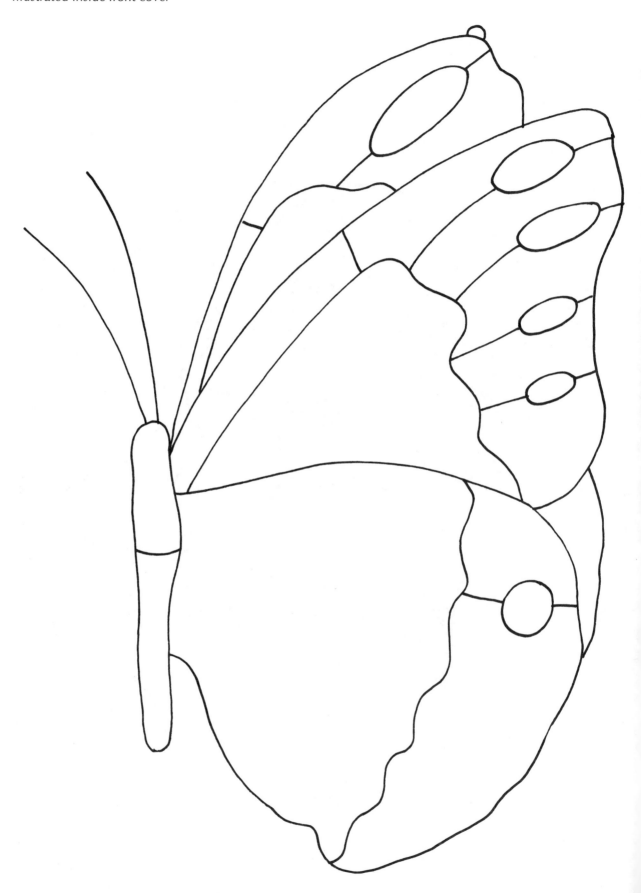

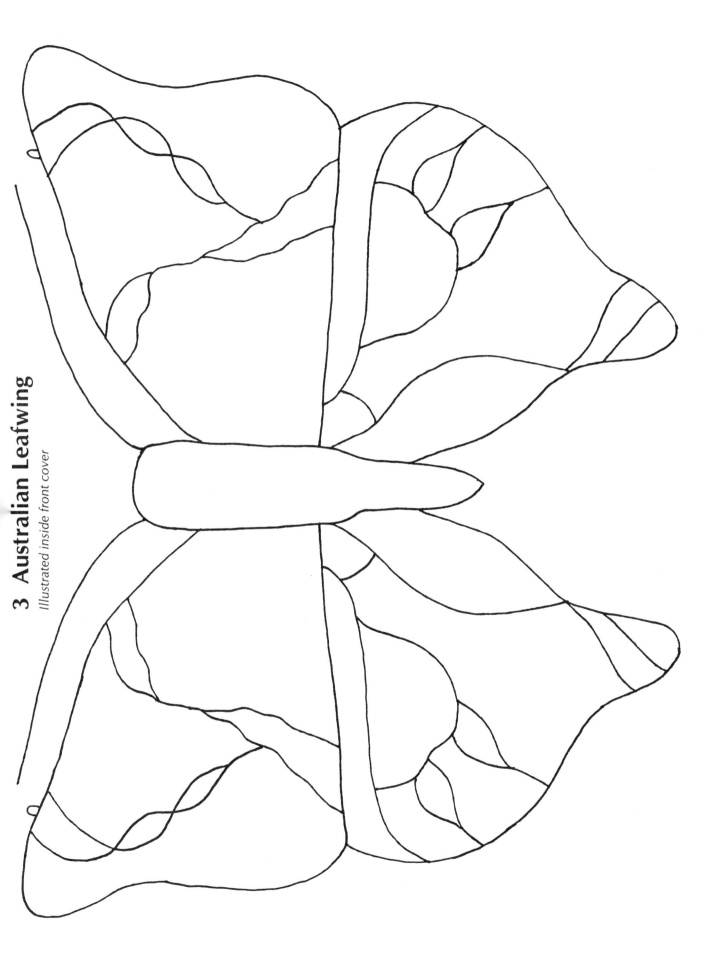

3 Australian Leafwing
Illustrated inside front cover

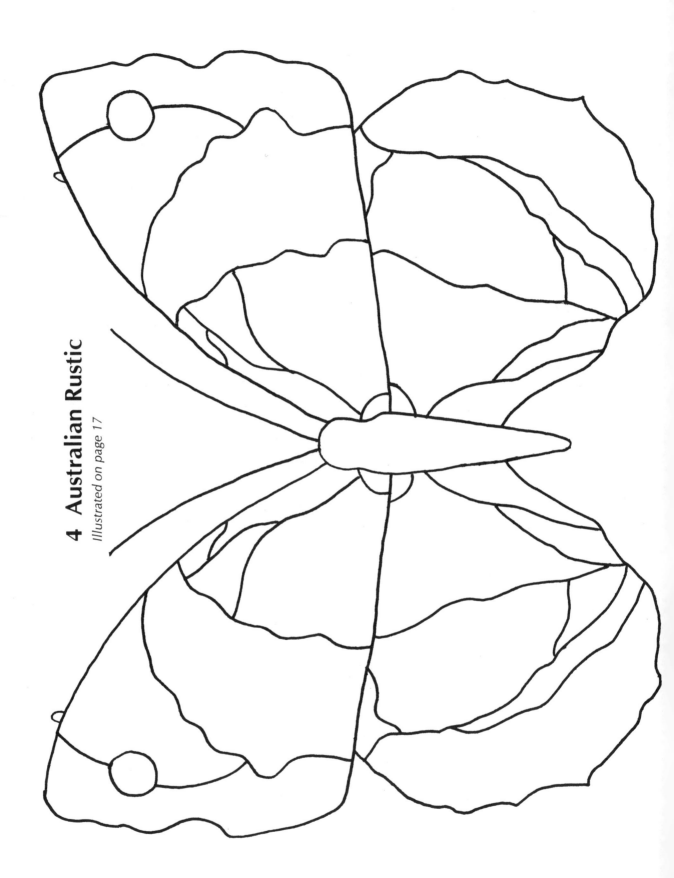

4 Australian Rustic
Illustrated on page 17

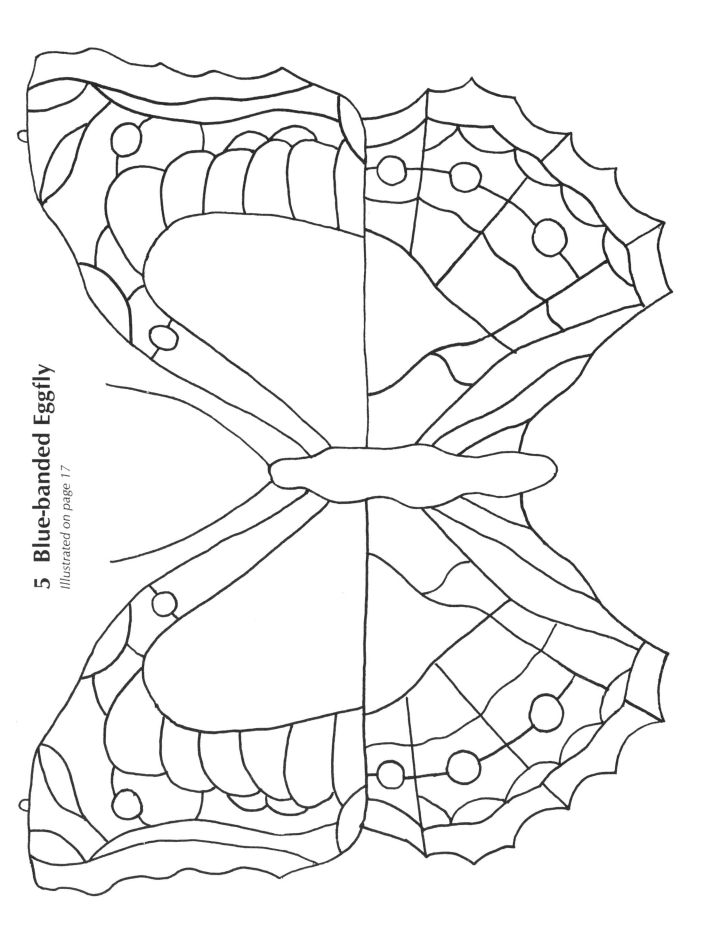

5 Blue-banded Eggfly

Illustrated on page 17

6 Blue Triangle

Illustrated on page 17

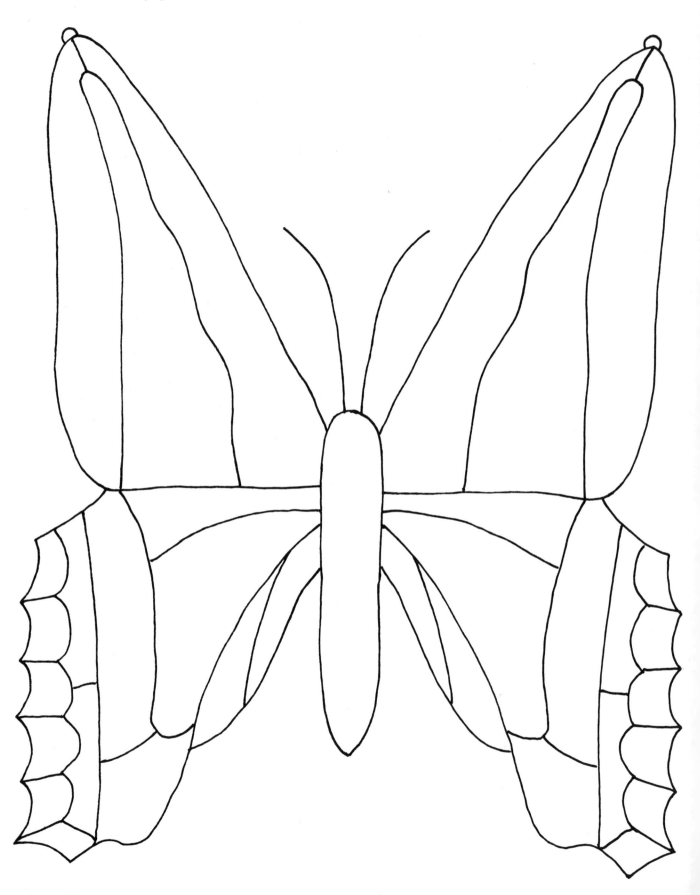

7 Broad-margined Grass Yellow and Marigolds

Illustrated on page 17

**8 Butterflies
with Native Fuchsia**

Illustrated on page 18

4 Australian Rustic

5 Blue-banded Eggfly

6 Blue Triangle

7 Broad-margined Grass Yellow and Marigolds

17

11 Common Eggfly

8 Butterflies with Native Fuchsia

9 Cairns Birdwing

10 Common Albatross and fruit

12 Common Eggfly and Flannel Flowers

13 Common Grass Yellow

15 Common Oakblue

14 Common Grass Yellow and flowers

19

16 Common Tit

17 Copper Jewel

18 Dingy Swallowtail

19 Fruhstorfer and Mexican Poppy

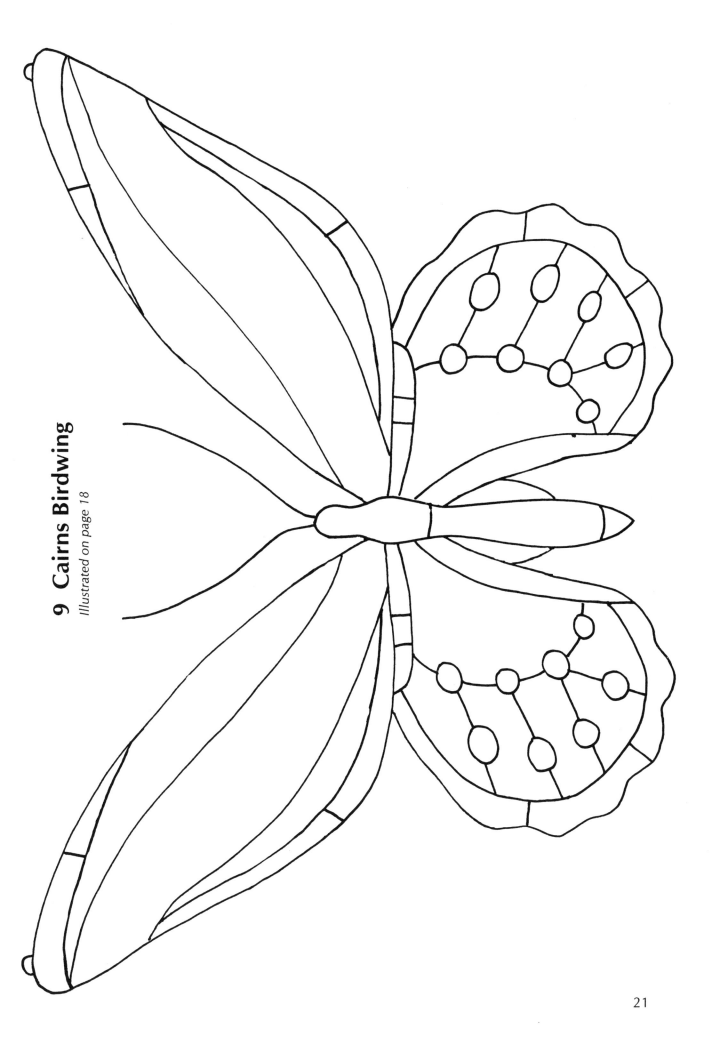

9 Cairns Birdwing

Illustrated on page 18

10 Common Albatross and fruit

Illustrated on page 18

11 Common Eggfly

Illustrated on page 18

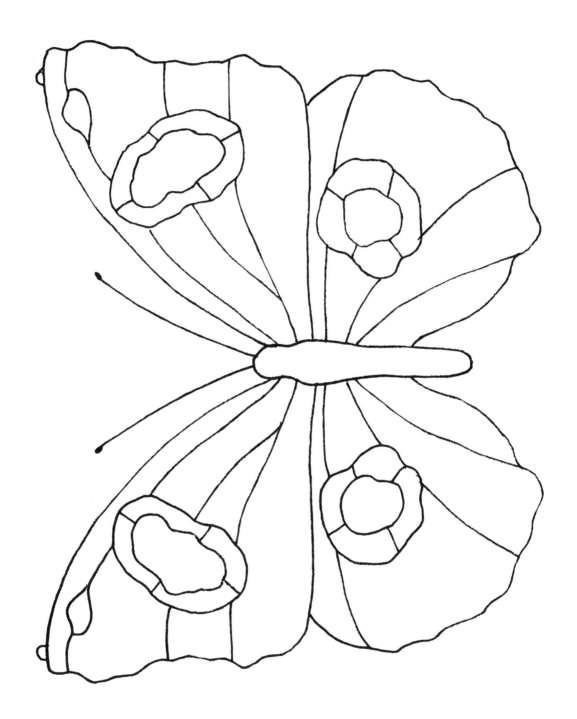

12 Common Eggfly and Flannel Flowers

Illustrated on page 19

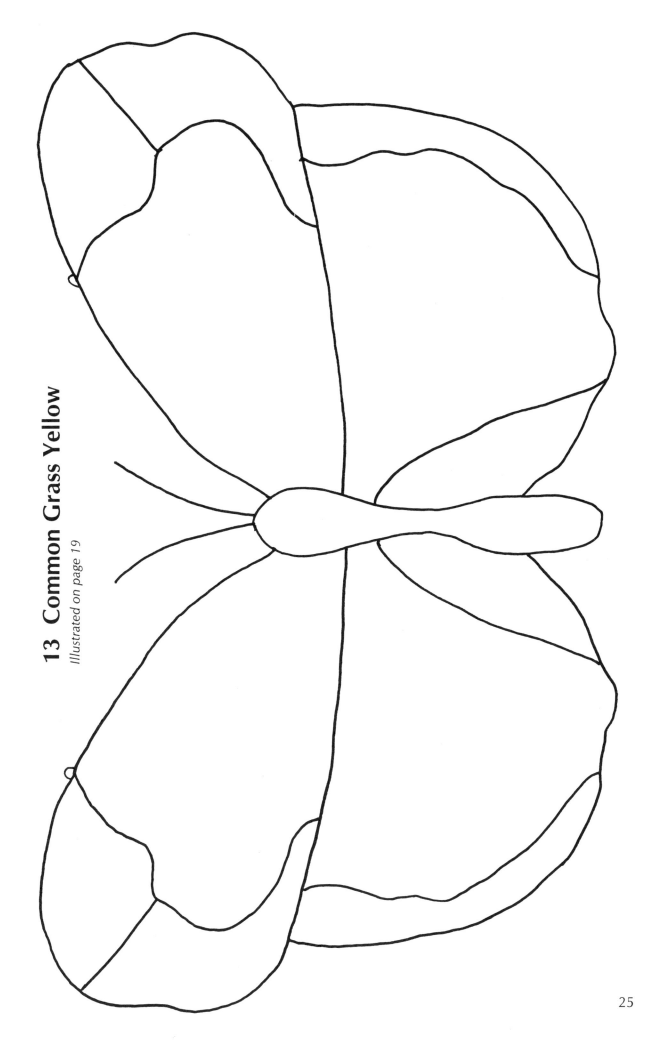

13 Common Grass Yellow

Illustrated on page 19

14 Common Grass Yellow and flowers

Illustrated on page 19

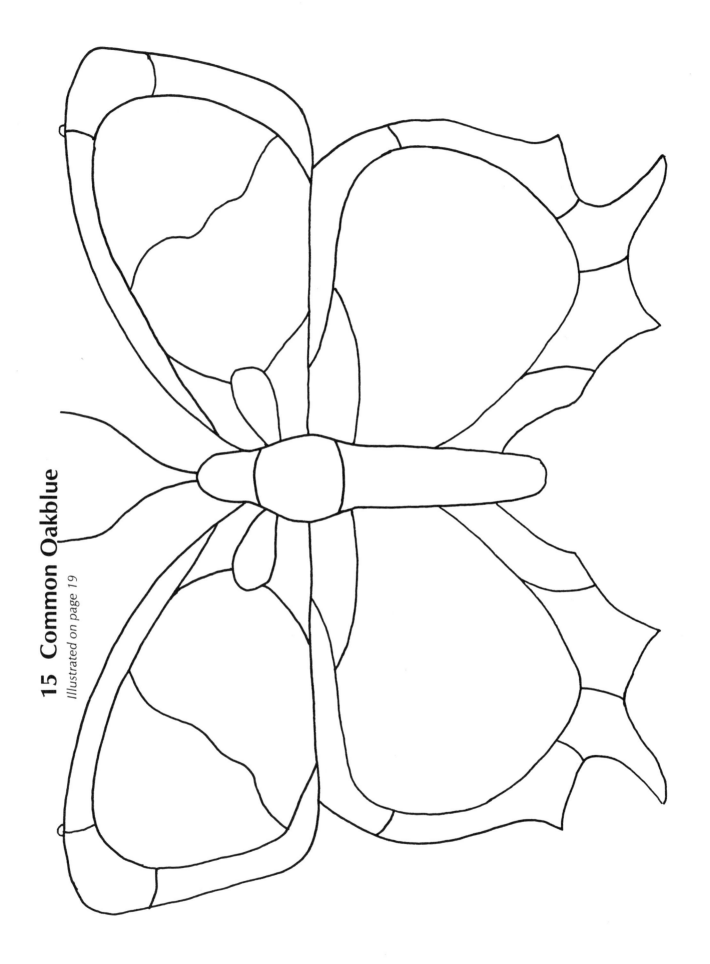

15 Common Oakblue

Illustrated on page 19

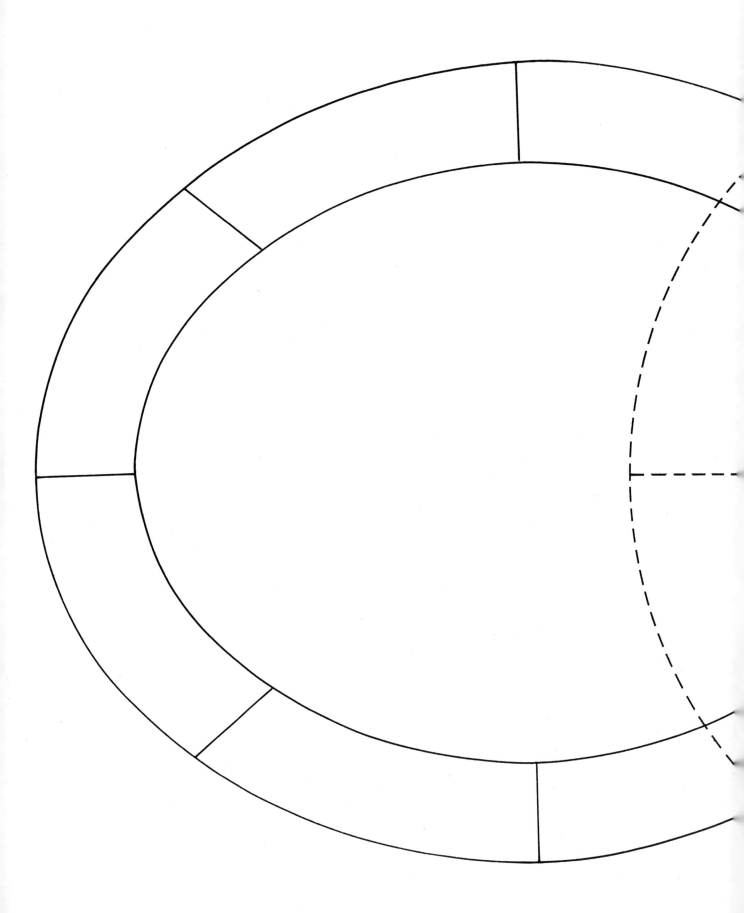

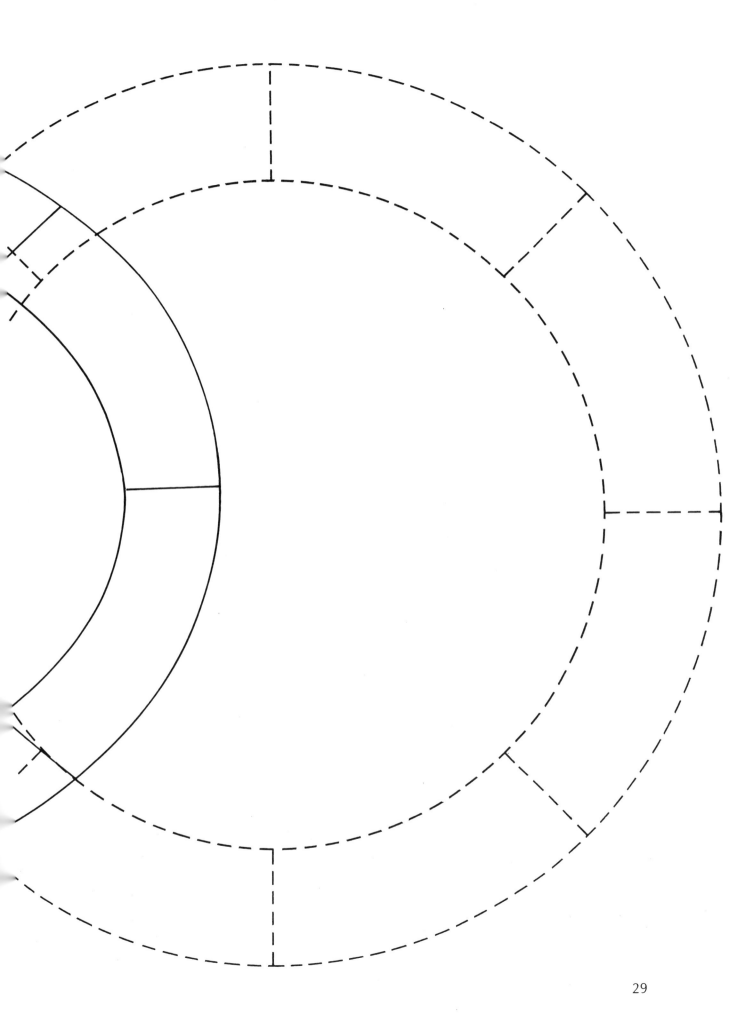

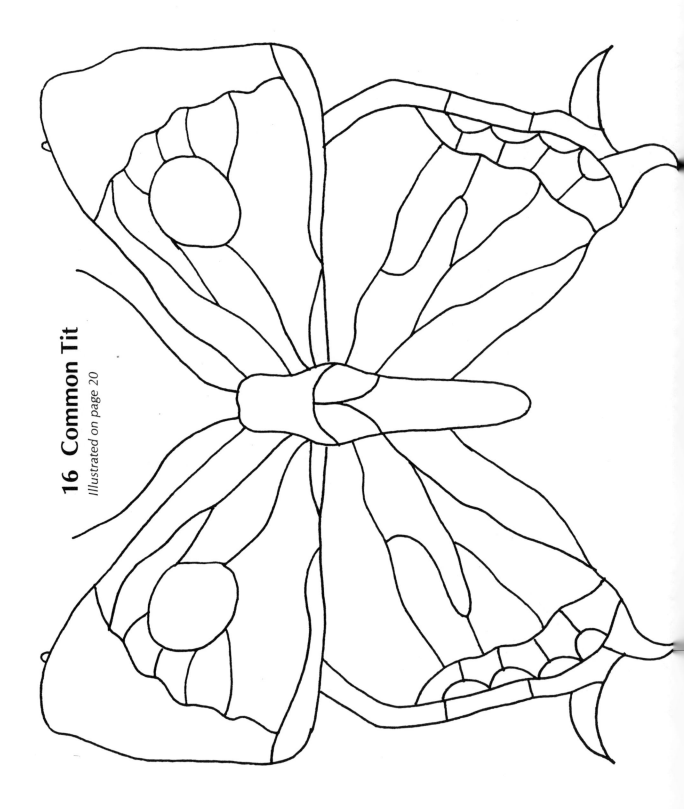

16 Common Tit

Illustrated on page 20

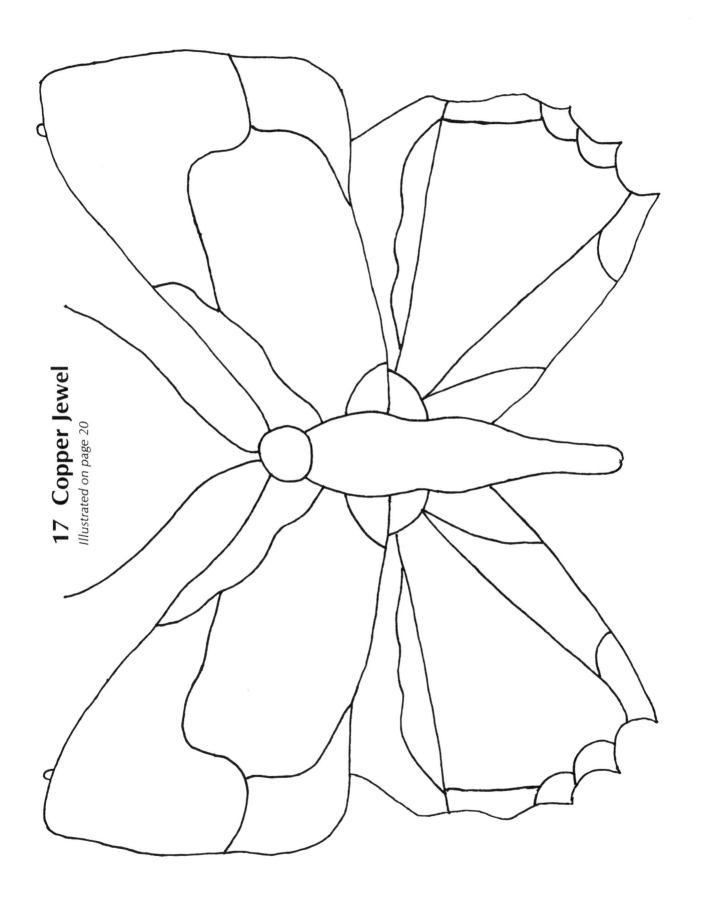

17 Copper Jewel
Illustrated on page 20

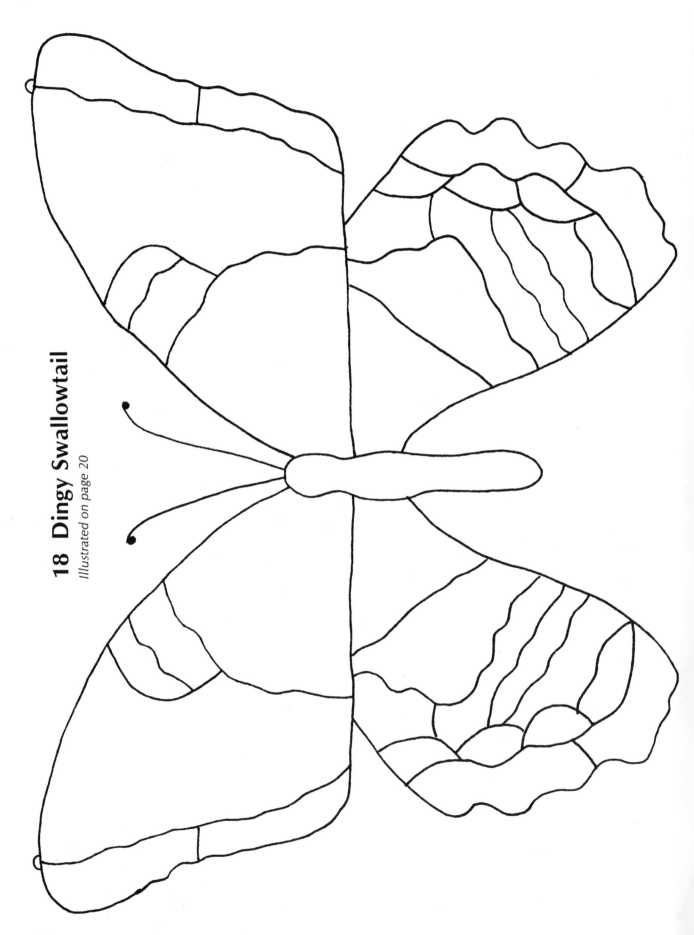

18 Dingy Swallowtail
Illustrated on page 20

Illustrated on page 20

19 Fruhstorfer and Mexican Poppy

20 Goddart

Illustrated on page 37

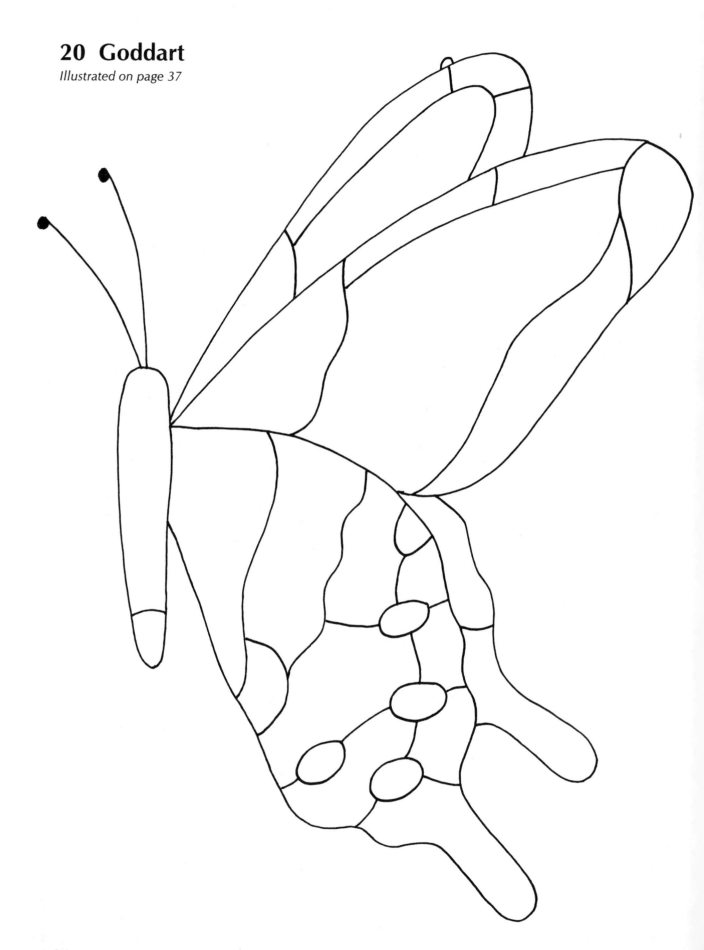

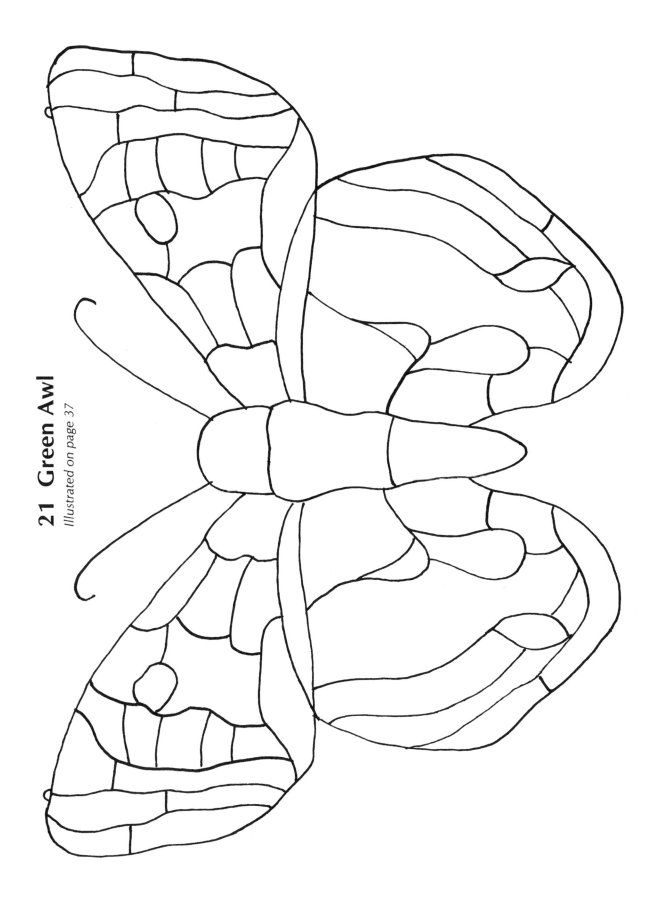

21 Green Awl

Illustrated on page 37

22 Hewitson

Illustrated on page 37

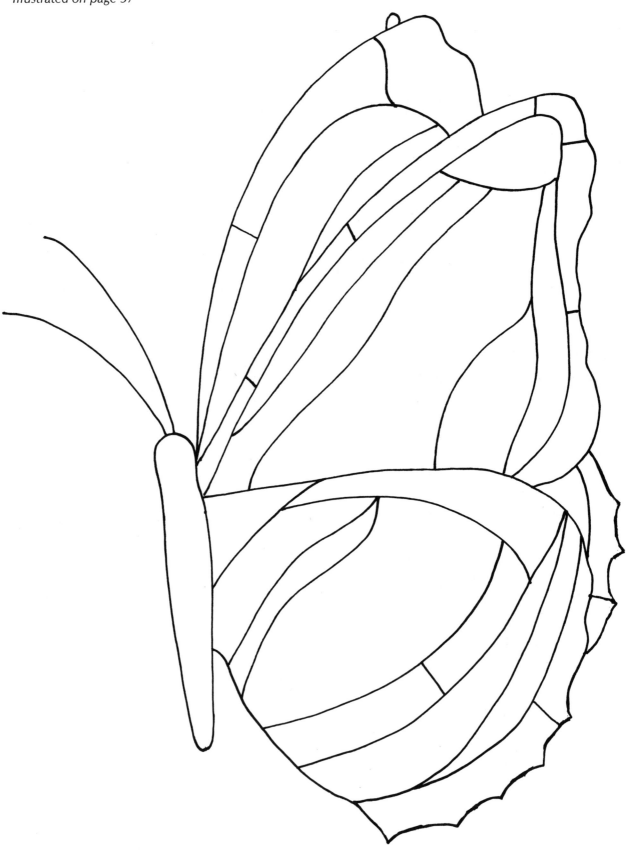

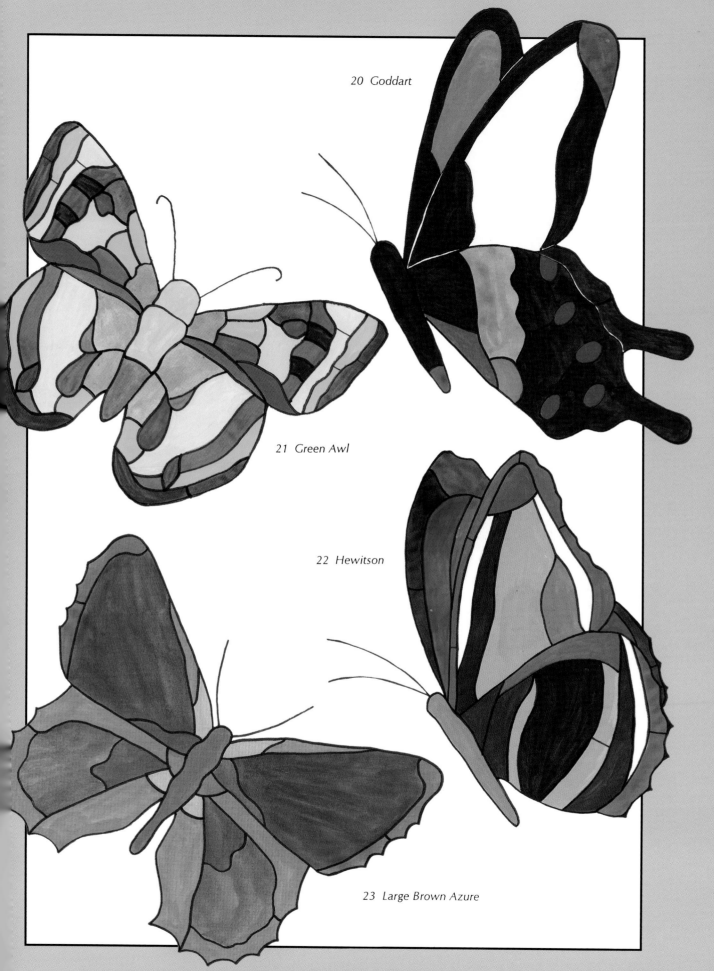

20 Goddart

21 Green Awl

22 Hewitson

23 Large Brown Azure

26 Monarch and Mexican Poppy

24 Large Green-banded Blue

25 Monarch

27 Narcissus Jewel

28 Northern Jezabel

29 Orange Lacewing

30 Plain Tiger

31 Red Lacewing

32 Regent Skipper

33 Silky Azure

34 Small Brown Azure

35 Ulysses Mountain Blue

40

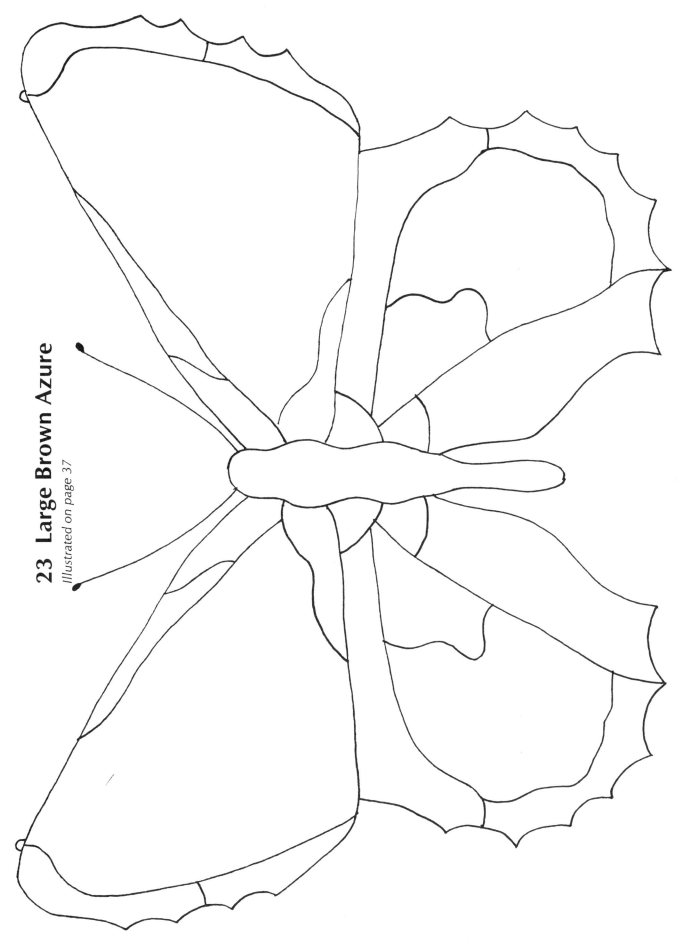

23 Large Brown Azure

Illustrated on page 37

24 Large Green-banded Blue

Illustrated on page 38

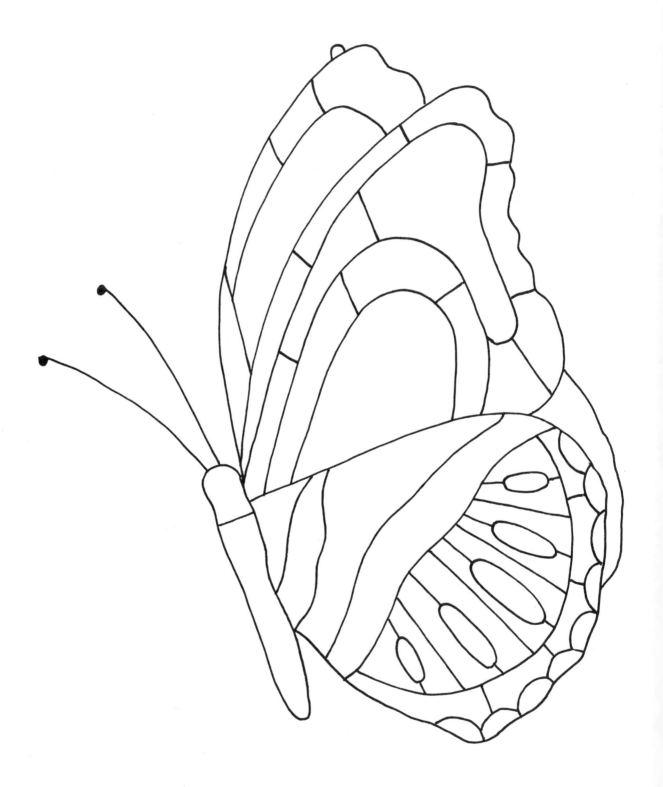

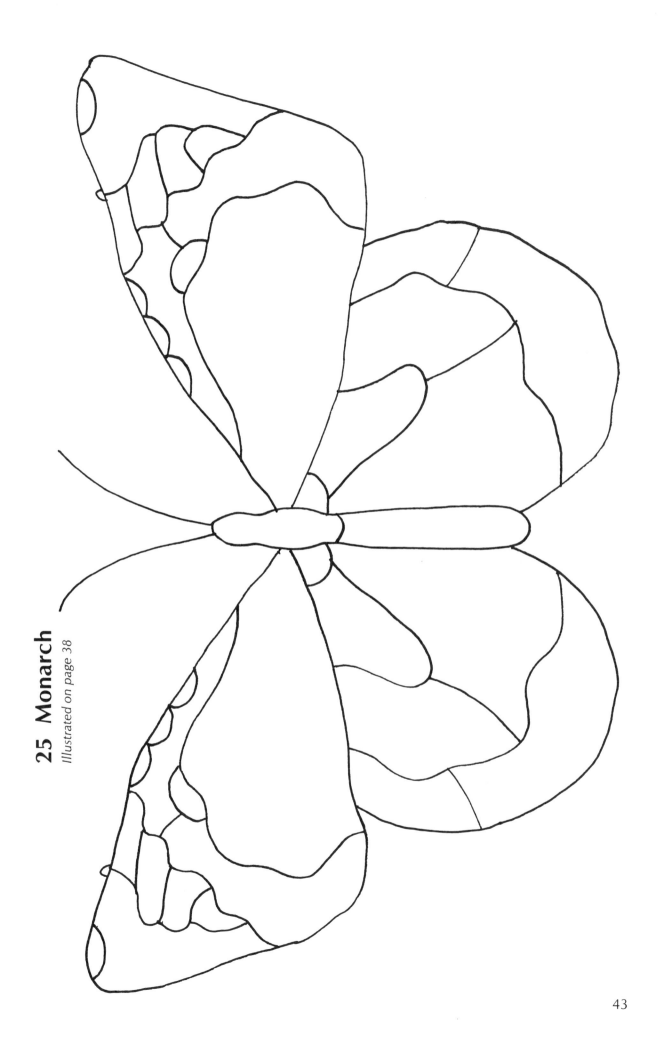

25 Monarch
Illustrated on page 38

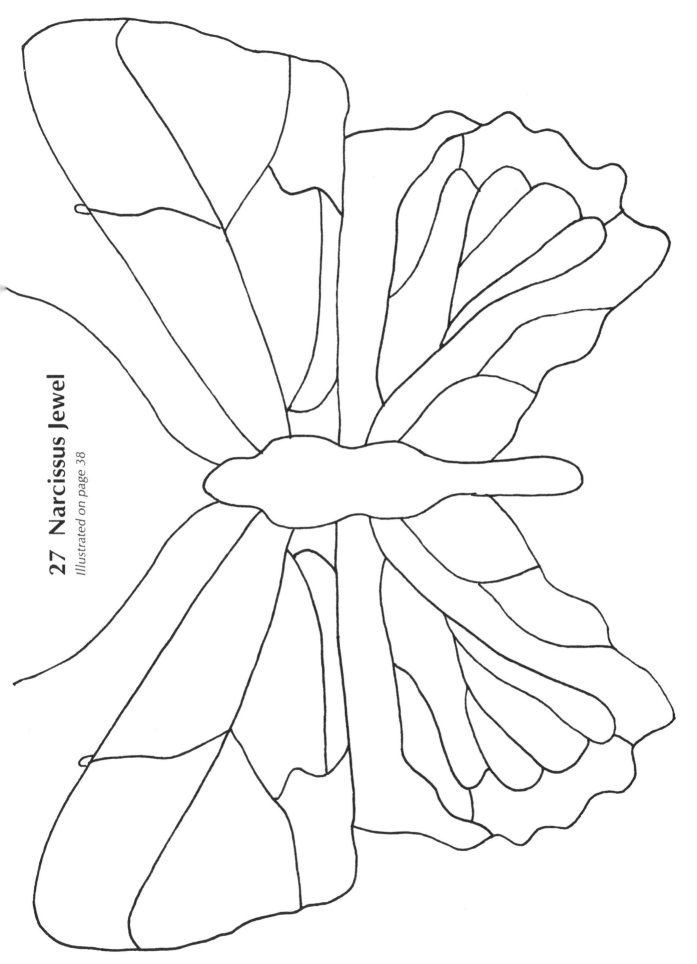

27 Narcissus Jewel
Illustrated on page 38

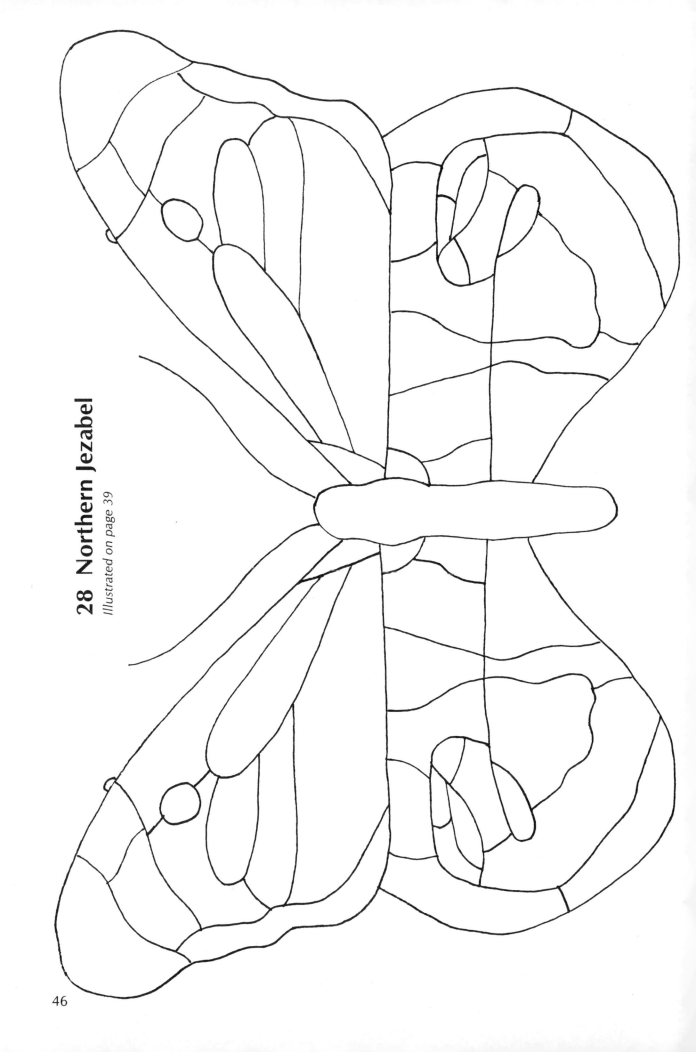

28 Northern Jezabel

Illustrated on page 39

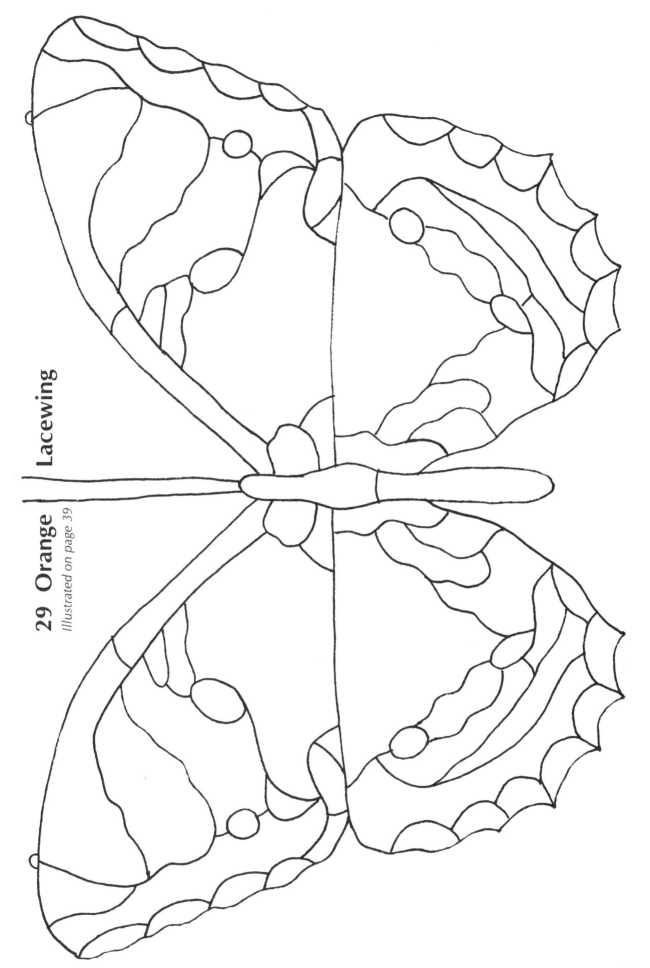

29 Orange | **Lacewing**
Illustrated on page 39

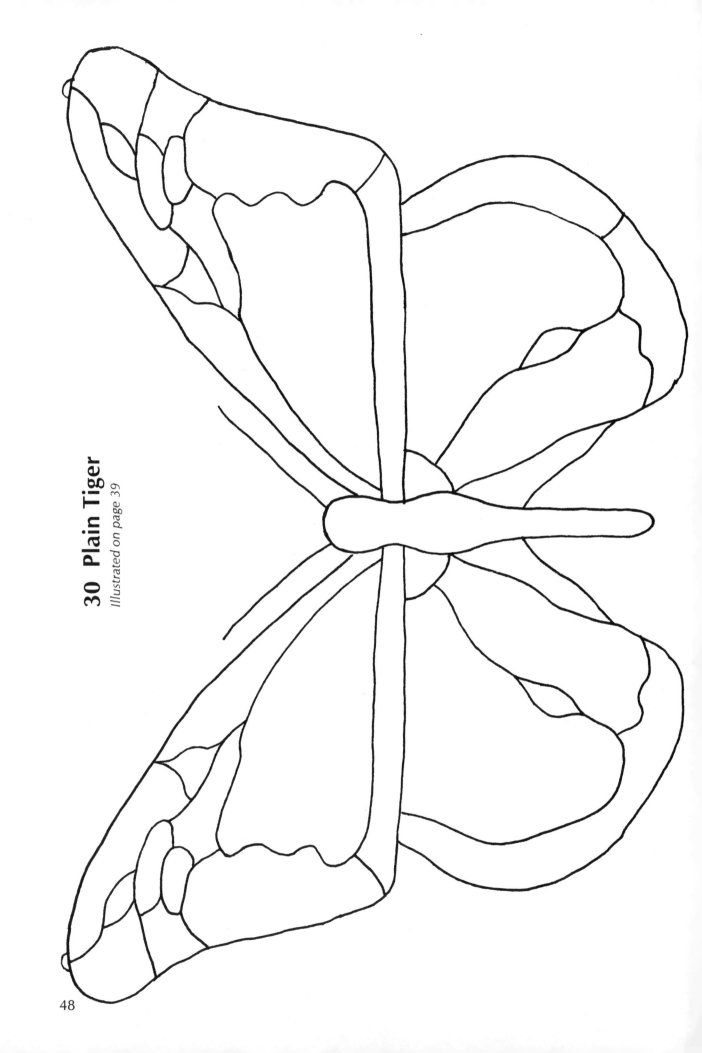

30 Plain Tiger
Illustrated on page 39

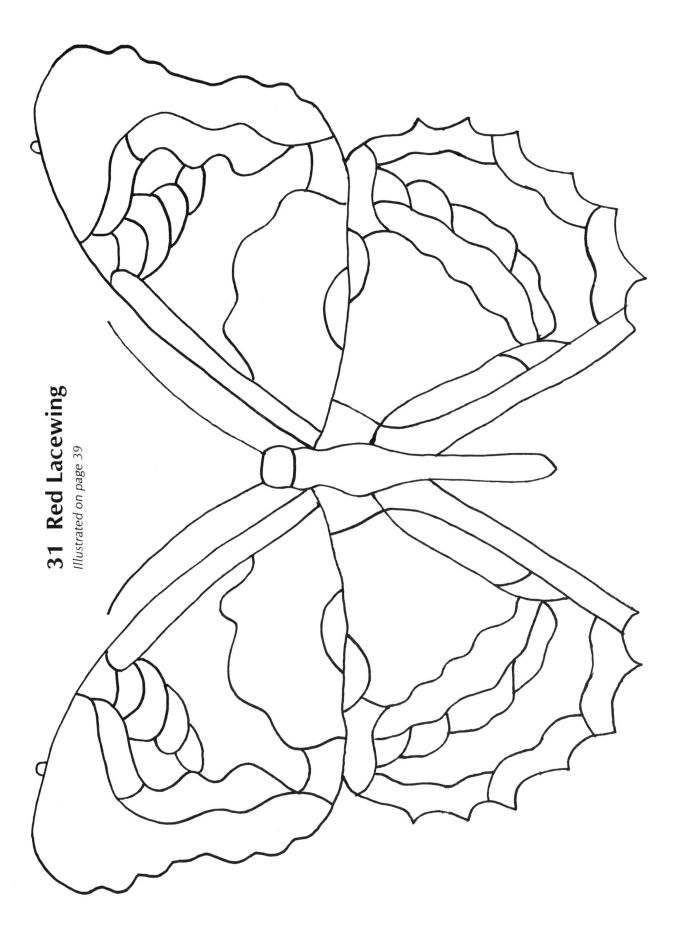

31 Red Lacewing
Illustrated on page 39

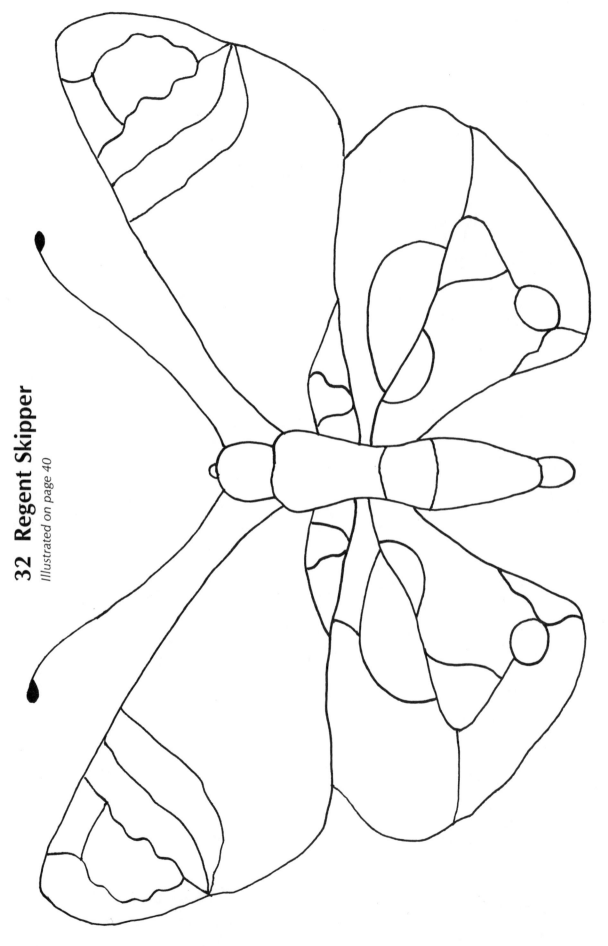

32 Regent Skipper
Illustrated on page 40

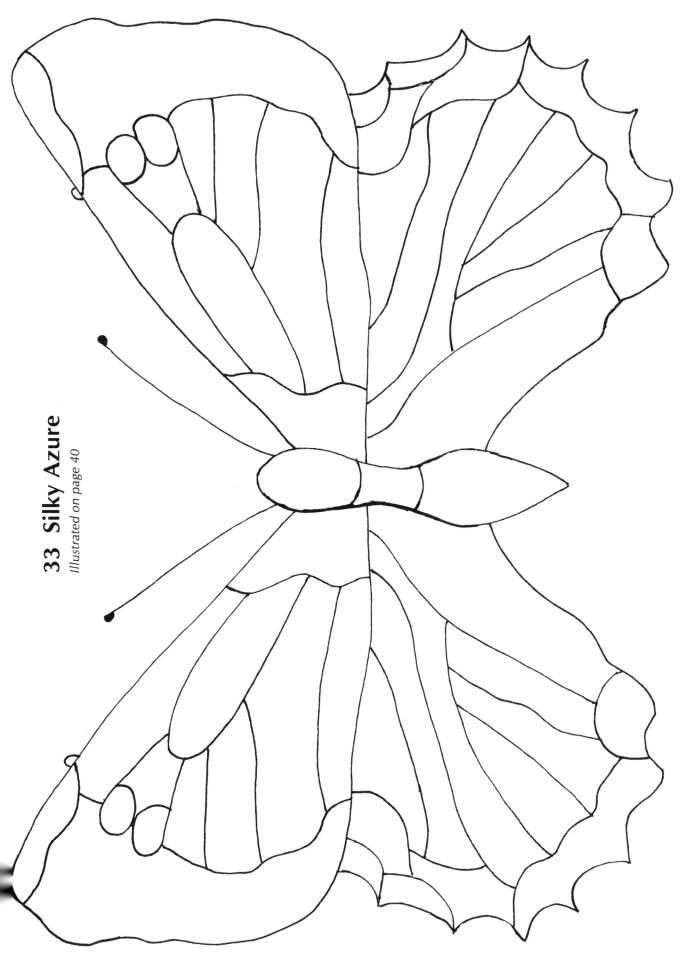

33 Silky Azure
Illustrated on page 40

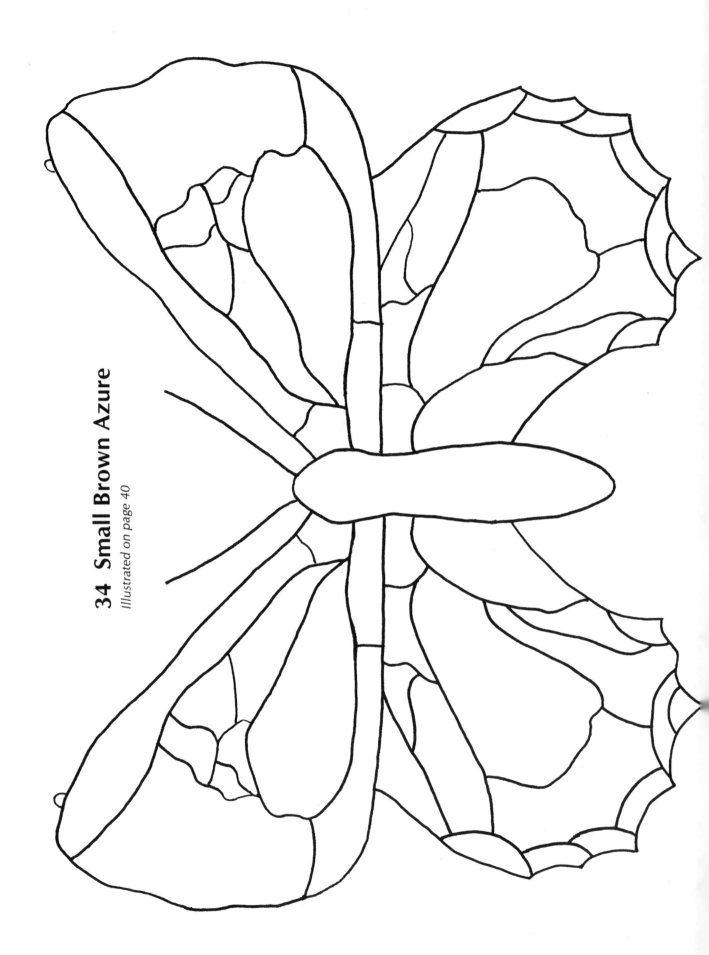

34 Small Brown Azure

Illustrated on page 40

35 Ulysses Mountain Blue
Illustrated on page 40

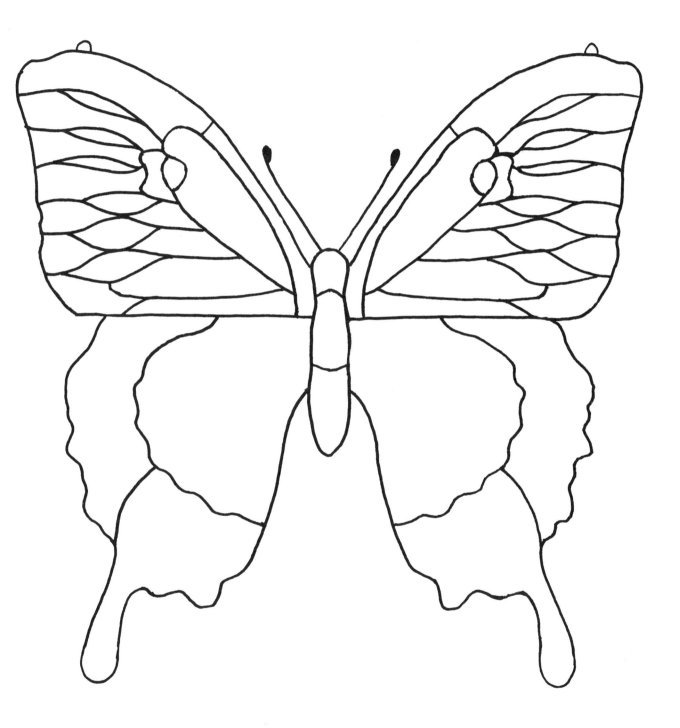

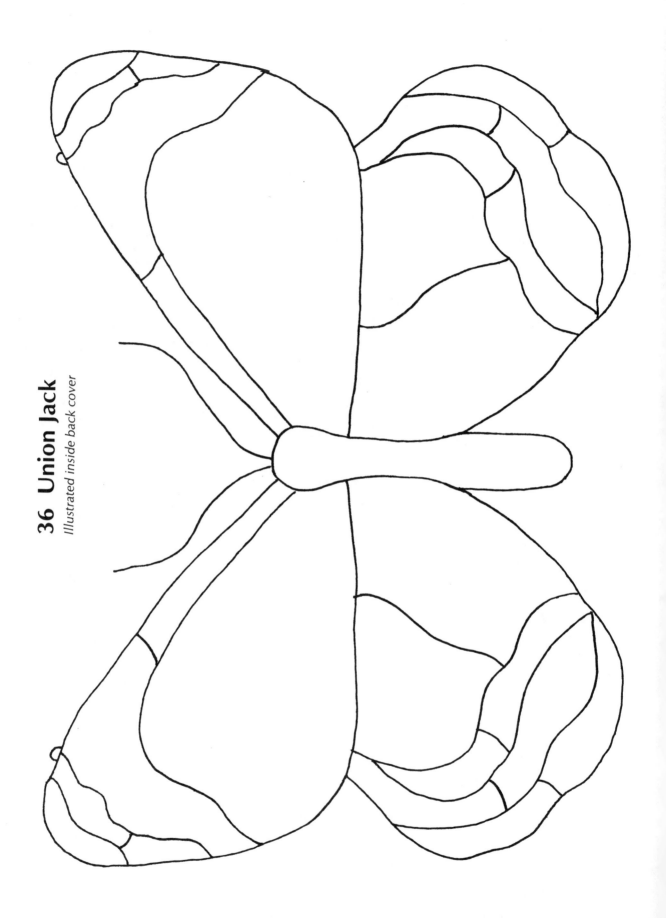

36 Union Jack
Illustrated inside back cover

37 White Nymph and Myrtle-leaf Milkwort

Illustrated inside back cover

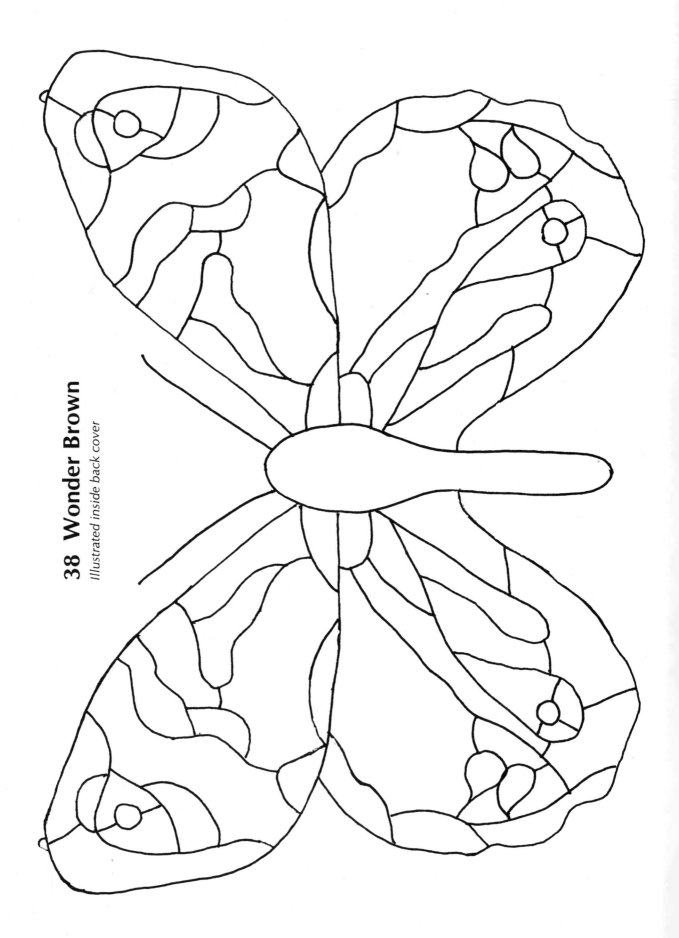

38 Wonder Brown
Illustrated inside back cover